Should I Go to College?

What about Student Loan Debt?

A Former Teacher's Guide to Possibly Saving You Thousands of Dollars and Millions of Headaches

(AND I'VE WRITTEN IT ALL DOWN TO MAKE IT EASY FOR YOU!)

MRS. JOHNSON

Copyright © 2019 by C. S. Johnson.
Publication: March 14, 2019

Price: $9.99 US

ALL PROCEEDS FROM THIS BOOK WILL BE USED TO HELP STUDENTS PAY DOWN STUDENT LOAN DEBT. Sign up for my mailing list for more information at https://www.csjohnson.me!

All rights reserved. This book or any portion thereof may not be reproduced or used in any manner whatsoever without the express written permission of the publisher.

eBOOK ISBN: 978-1-948464-29-1

PAPERBACK ISBN: 978-1-948464-30-7

TABLE OF CONTENTS

If, in the event you cannot find what you are looking for, please read the chapter titles.

PREFACE

CHAPTER 1: WHAT IS COLLEGE, AND WHY SHOULD YOU PAY FOR IT?

CHAPTER 2: STUDENT DEBT IN AMERICA

CHAPTER 3: THE CASE FOR COLLEGE

CHAPTER 4: COLLEGE OPTION #1: NO

CHAPTER 5: COLLEGE OPTION #2: NOT YET

CHAPTER 6: COLLEGE OPTION #3: YES, VARIATION ONE

CHAPTER 7: COLLEGE OPTION #4: YES, VARIATION TWO

CHAPTER 8: COLLEGE OPTION #5: YES, VARIATION THREE

CHAPTER 9: COLLEGE OPTION #6: YES, NON-TRADITIONAL

CHAPTER 10: PROACTIVE TIPS (NOT THE ACNE KIND)

CHAPTER 11: REACTIVE TIPS (NOT THE RADIOACTIVE KIND)

CHAPTER 12: CLOSING STATEMENTS

ABOUT THE AUTHOR

AUTHOR'S NOTE

AUTHOR'S ACKNOWLEDGEMENTS

PREFACE

I WAS A TEACHER FOR A QUITE A LONG time. I taught for about eight years, and while that might not seem like much, I can assure you that eight years is a *long* time -- made even more so because . . . it's teaching. The teaching profession in America is on the decline (I have made it a personal mission to make sure my children are not teachers, and I know I am not alone in this), and I am not the only one who has blamed more paperwork and more bureaucracy for this situation.

Having firsthand knowledge, I can't blame teachers for quitting. One can only take hearing the same excuses so many times ("My grandmother was in the hospital," "My computer got a virus," "My family was eaten by a raging pack of rabid squirrels who'd gotten into my neighbor's secret cannabis farm," etc.) before taking it personally. Of course you take it personally! It's not like the actual insults -- both to your face and behind your back -- with all the implied and direct barbs, haven't gotten to you. Nor has the disingenuous interest or the genuine apathy escaped your notice. Not to mention the rise of terrible administrators, the lack of a real support system, and the way so much pressure is put on students to work with computers and science. (Did you know that since STEM majors are the current "IT girl" ha! in education, English and History teachers also have to include assignments that touch on those subjects?) That's not the only area, either. Since the culture is so obsessed with sex, it usually comes up in our conversations. I've had students asking if Louis XVI was gay or if Marshmallow Man was asexual, if Picard from that one *Star Trek* TV show had more or less sex than the average person because he was bald.

But yes . . . multiple subjects are inserted into the topical classes just so we can pretend we're doing right by our professional duties.

So, as a teacher, you feel like the job you pursued in hopes of getting to talk to the next generation about your love of poetry or your obsession with historical dates has turned into a sales job, and you couldn't care less about the product. There's a reason an AT&T salesman won't try to sell you cable while also offering you a discount on a treadmill and a free mounted animal head for your bathroom.

Teachers today are largely overworked, underpaid, underappreciated, and overstressed. It's easier to believe we can throw money at a problem to fix it, but that's not true. You actually have to have people show up, and teaching is automatically handicapped, because the people who have to show up include students, parents, and sometimes the police or a social worker. And at any given moment, at least two of those three parties don't come or don't really want to come.

Being a teacher in today's world means choosing to be the George Costanza of career choices. (No offense, Jason Alexander.) You're always upset about something that may or may not be your fault, you feel awkward and ugly and looked down on, and so much of other people's lives and good humor depends on you.

This has been my experience as a teacher. I was a teacher for eight years. The average number of years a teacher spends teaching in the classroom is five. *Five*.

Why did I stay for so long? Stockholm syndrome comes to mind.

I also went to college, with my parents spending an obscene amount of money for my tuition while I personally borrowed more. During these years, I went to class, and worked through endless piles of paperwork, all with bloated hopes and lofty goals of "changing the world" and "making the world a better place."

Now, I don't want to teach anymore. I'm good at it, and I know what to do and how to do it, but I don't want to teach anymore. If I only remain in the profession for five years, it's a sad ROI (return on investment—brush up on your finance lingo, we're going to have more complicated words in a few moments.) And this matters to me.

There is a reasonable stereotype out there that teachers are frugal. It took me about $60,000 to get through college. My parents saved a good portion of that money as I was growing up. I borrowed the rest of it and worked while I was in school to pay it off. But seriously, that means I spent between $15,000 and $20,000 *a year* to find out I hate what I do. I could have been happier borrowing that money to build a house in the woods and paying for lessons on hunting at the archery range.

There's not only the money factor to consider. Or even the happiness factor. There's the stress factor too. I probably lost years of my life worrying about silly things like calling parents, meeting with administrators, making sure I CC'd the right people in emails, and making sure the coffee pot was full.

Some days I still I wish I could have lasted longer. Maybe if more people had taken me seriously, and maybe if I had taken the job *less* seriously … Maybe if I could have had a taxidermy animal, bleached white and bound up with rusty chains next to my desk and called it "Marley," the profession would hold less negative Scrooge-like magic for me. Of course, one of the students would have used my Marley to stash his drugs, or another student would have carved the chains into daggers when I wasn't looking.

SIDE NOTE #1: Do you know how hard it is to write on the board and keep your eyes on twenty-five-plus puberty-ridden children/wannabe adults, all experiencing the varying range of emotions portrayed on all that lovely American television? Frankly, it's a wonder America does *so well* on their international exams. That, and China probably has better methods of cheating than we do. If they had gunpowder before us, they probably figured out the SAT answer key before us, too. Russia or Japan might have it, too, though Japan probably replaced their population of school children with androids. Russia's got Dr. No, so I bet they have computer mesh-nets for brain enhancement surgeries ready to go somewhere. My next bet would be the Republic of Chad, because they're just too quiet. And it's always the quiet ones, right? But I digress.

So I have automatically earned an "A" in teaching, (especially if we're using the American grading system, which has been experiencing some inflation in recent years and that alone should qualify me to write this book, and for you to take everything I say in it extremely seriously. I officially earned my right to be a dinosaur in the teaching field, so hear me *roar!* If nothing else, that might keep you awake long enough to read it. (I just read an article today about how students can't read full textbooks anymore, and it's largely because they don't have the attention spans to do so.)

Chances are you've picked this book up because you've read my other books, or because you know someone or want someone—someone who may live in your basement or spare room or backyard—to consider going off to college. And that might be a very good idea. Or it could be a very bad idea. We live in a strange age, where the end justifies the means, even when it is not supposed to.

Do I regret going to college and getting my degree? Despite my earlier rant, the answer is no. I do regret making it the be-all-end-all of my life at the time. I actually laughed at a one of my college students who told me she was worried her GPA would drop because she got a B for the first time in one of her classes. She didn't think it was funny, but *I* thought it was funny. I used to feel the exact same way about my grades, but one class grade ultimately didn't matter much. (It is most college's policy that a student will be able to retake a class if he or she is not satisfied with the grade, but is most likely not worth the effort or the cost.)

I thought college was my ticket to happiness, but it wasn't. Turns out, I wanted to be a writer. You don't need to go to college for that. You don't need to go to grad school for that either, even though Stephanie Meyer did.

SIDE NOTE #2: Maybe I should have included Vampires in this book.

But anyway, I do not regret my degree in education. Not entirely.

I learned a lot about people during that time. I learned that textbook companies have been updating their books and changing the terminology for things needlessly at an increasing rate to make sure students pay the most money for their books. I learned that professors with doctorates have a lot less work to grade than the professors who only have their master's degrees. I learned that there's so much information that there's not enough money, even from your inflated tuition rates at college, to pay for all the people who need to keep track of it. (That's why the government steps in, apparently.) I learned that people really change once you've bought what they are selling. I learned how people who are in charge for too long forget to listen. How old people don't understand young people. And how you think you're smart until someone smarter comes along, and you forget the difference between smart and smart-sounding long enough to play mind games with yourself. (Spoiler: You'll lose even if you win when you play against yourself.)

I didn't just learn this from watching it while I was in college. I taught at a college, too. I've learned a few tricks that can help, that you most likely know or can Google, but I can confirm with real-world experience.

As a teacher, I have been trained to read people as students and analyze them for weaknesses, strengths, skills, emotional and intellectual development, and motivation. I can help you save yourself the time and energy and stress when it comes to college and student loans. This book is part of a my effort to raise awareness and critical thinking (so you know it'll only be a bestseller if some famous, bone-headed schmuck likes it) when it comes to deciding if college is right for you, and paying off student loan debt should you decide to journey into the world of academia.

ALL PROCEEDS FROM THIS BOOK WILL BE USED TO HELP STUDENTS PAY DOWN STUDENT LOAN DEBT.

I'd love to be able to help others pay down their student loan debts. *You* can help by buying this book, at its regular price, and encouraging your friends and family to buy it as well.

With the United States government's current policies, many students are able to pay between $50-500 a month toward their balances. I'm writing this book to help students, workers, and families get some extra help. This is for US students only right now, but if I ever do get my dreams of starting a charity off the ground, I'd love to take this to the rest of the world.

Help me slay the dragon of student debt in America, one student at a time. The only good debt is a debt that's paid. Don't let anyone tell you otherwise.

Your Loving Teacher,

Mrs. Johnson

CHAPTER 1: WHAT IS COLLEGE, AND WHY SHOULD YOU PAY FOR IT?

I DON'T LIKE TO SPLIT HAIRS, BUT THIS IS A rare, unfortunate instance where it needs to be done. You can ask 20 people on the street what college is, and they'll most likely agree that it's a place where you go and pay a lot of money to learn stuff. But when you ask what those 20 people *did* at college, they'll likely give you significantly different answers. I did not actually do this because, come on, I interact with enough people on a daily basis. Don't make me reach out to more when I'm not actually being paid to, or when no one is threatening me with a stick or something. Some might say that my take on things is somewhat cynical. I tell them I am "enlightened."

So, what is college?

College, with its various levels of administrators, professors, and other people they hire with all the grant money from either government sources or private foundations, is a well-oiled, bureaucratic machine, designed with the thought of preventing students from suing it.

Syllabi become the contract by which you operate. Assignments are listed, rules are explained, and standards are presented. It's up to you to do the work to meet the expectations they give you for the grade you want. Many students try to challenge this with cries for extra credit, but that's usually because they have not done any of the work in question.

Instructors are retained if they have good survey results—a favorable rating by other professors and students—and if they don't cause too much uproar on their respective campuses. The material for each class is (usually) outlined, so even if the teacher varies, there is some cohesiveness to the curriculum.

You also usually have a dorm room which you'll share with someone who will learn very quickly how to make your life a living hell, and if it is in his or her best interest to avoid that or not.

Many campuses have sports teams, or they are in the process of getting sports teams. Either way, it's a good excuse to slap an extra $100+ on your tuition bill. Technology is vastly different, but the money for the tech fees largely does the same thing.

There is always a cafeteria, which will allow the college to make you pay for food you will grow to hate with a surprising passion, unless you are very, very, very fortunate.

I've even heard that there are several "classes" now on silly, impractical things that are more politically driven. (Save your money here. Go travel to a poor country and see how people live in refugee camps or destitute nations; go see the inner city, where drugs and gangs and death abound. You'll see how far you are already, no matter where you've come from.)

EDUCATION ALONE WON'T CHANGE PEOPLE'S HEARTS. IT'LL CHANGE THEIR

HEADS, BUT YOU NEED MORE IF YOU'RE GOING TO CHANGE SOMEONE'S HABITS.

Education alone won't change people's hearts. It'll change their heads, but you need more if you're going to change someone's habits. It doesn't take a class to teach you that to live in America is to be fortunate. It does, however, take a socio-political movement, closely tied to educational funding, to find a way to profit from it.

So that's college.

Now, why should you pay for it?

WHY SHOULD YOU PAY FOR COLLEGE?

Colleges have access to professionals who teach. These people are called "professors." They have experience and education that will help you, no matter what field you want to study. They teach these things in "classes," which will also likely include a list of resources where you can learn more (though on your own time) and will guide you in understanding the fundamentals of your chosen career path.

Teachers should be paid. For all the "free college" stuff I hear, I do not hear how teachers, instructors, and professors should be paid. Your tuition helps pay for that access, put toward a wage that will help the professor afford a living space, a working space, or internet access.

That's reasonable.

You, as a student, also have access to benefits as a member of the campus you are on, or the one that you sign onto via the internet.

You get a new email address (a professional-sounding email can make all the difference; I don't want to hire "Hotguyz4me22222@male.com" unless I am looking for a pimp. And given that I have never tried to contact one, I am sure even pimps have better sounding emails than the one I just made up). You get access to many books and research and journals on campus as well as online. (Thank God for virtual libraries!) Your teachers can often provide references for the future, when you apply to jobs.

That is also reasonable.

There's another benefit as well; one that I never took much advantage of: networking.

Your peers, especially the ones that you work with in college, have priorities similar to yours. You want to create your own business? In a business program, you could have 30+ people all working to start their own businesses, and you can learn a lot from their mistakes and their triumphs. You want to start your own business after thirty years have passed since college? Chances are you could easily reach out to old colleagues and see if there's a way they can help you.

Networking is critical in a lot of today's businesses. Many people often get a job because they "know the right people." And jobs are not the only things that come from knowing the right people.

When I was in high school, I had a friend who knew a member of the Rotary Club International. My friend talked with the club member and, three months later, my friend had a scholarship that paid for half of her college tuition.

I know another person who wanted to work for a company in another city. He knew someone from school who worked there, so he was able to get an interview and later got the job.

As a teacher, I played this role several times myself; if I have students who would make a good fit in a business I have a connection with, I'll pass along their resumes or fill out a reference form.

So, yes. Networking *matters*.

It is reasonable to pay for that as well.

That being said, there is a limit to reason -- which we'll discuss in the next chapter.

CHAPTER RECAP:

1. College is a business that brings teachers, supplies, resources, and students together for a variety of activities, all geared toward making money while helping people learn.
2. Meal plans have a dark side.
3. There are *some* reasonable things to pay for at college that can lead to better jobs, better opportunities, etc.
4. Networking = essential.

TAKEAWAY:

1. Research the college you want to attend. Really, really, really research it. You don't want to waste your time or money on frivolous or downright stupid classes.
2. Once you're there, don't be a turd to your teachers or your peers. See how they can help you or how you can help them. (Generosity is *always* good.) Network and form friendships.
3. Get a professional email.

CHAPTER 2: STUDENT DEBT IN AMERICA
A Hot Mess

STUDENT LOAN DEBT IN AMERICA IS A quagmire. When it comes to problems, there are plenty of people who offer solutions – including some solutions that are pretty stupid, including ones that would add to the overall problem. Most of these people obviously don't work in the education system. Either that, or they are being bribed with incentives by lobbyists to sell out. But I'd hate to be *too* cynical here.

The aim of this book is to help students in America get out of student debt, which brings me to my first point: *The best way to get out of student loan debt is to AVOID getting into it in the first place.*

THE BEST WAY TO GET OUT OF STUDENT LOAN DEBT IS TO AVOID GETTING INTO IT IN THE FIRST PLACE.

Yes, yes, it seems simple enough for the average person to figure out. But it's often not logic that is the problem—it's emotional insecurity and poor self-discipline. I should know; I have years of impulse buying and an addiction to Diet Coke to prove I know what emotional insecurity and poor self-discipline look like.

And I taught people for a living, so I saw this pretty much every time I stepped into a classroom. So, there's that too.

So if the best way to get out of student loan debt is to avoid it, this means you can either NOT got to college, or you can go to college using a different path—one that requires a real plan, and not an I'll-just-wing-it-even-though-I-had-years-to-work-on-a-plan-but-I-need-it-in-the-next-twenty-minutes type of plan. I'll discuss those options in more detail in the next couple chapters, but first I wanted to present a more broad perspective on student loans in America. Good judgment requires a broad perspective. In this case, it begins with the following questions:

1. "Is college reasonable for me?
2. If so, which college is best for me and my education needs?
3. If not, what should I do?"

"IS COLLEGE REASONABLE FOR ME? IF SO, WHICH COLLEGE IS BEST FOR ME AND MY EDUCATION NEEDS? IF NOT, WHAT SHOULD I DO?"

In the last chapter, I mentioned how certain things in college are "reasonable." Reason is a tricky thing, because the line between "reasonable" and "not reasonable" can be blurry. Just look at *Gulliver's Travels*. The horse-people in the last land that he visited were *always* rational, but it led to inhumanity.

As of 2016, student loan debt in America is approximately 1.3 trillion dollars. That's straight from the studentloans.gov website. And that's just the government-funded loans. Private loans, from non-government-regulated places, are also hurting people.

Here's a way to look at it:

>1.3 Trillion dollars = $1,300,000,000,000
>1 Big Mac = ~ $3.50 / burger (average)
>1 Quadruple Bypass Surgery in America = $135,000

That means that you can ingest 371,428,532,857 Big Macs and still afford a quadruple bypass. That's enough to feed someone three meals a day for 123,809,510,952 days, which translates to over 300,000 years.

That's enough to make me lose my appetite while I'm writing this—at least enough to avoid McDonald's for lunch today.

With roughly 318.9 million people in America right now. With $1.3 trillion in debt, that breaks down into about $5,000 per person (not everyone has debt, of course). Not a lot of people just have $5,000 lying around. If you know someone who does, please pass this book to them. Given the price of some programs—which can vary between around $5,000-105,000+ a semester, depending on the school—it is even more unlikely that people will be able to afford college all at once.

This matters because there are studies that show the relationship between mental health and debt, and they find that the more debt you have, the more likely you are to be stressed, anxious, depressed, and have any number of complementary conditions.

Imagine this scenario: Depression leads to insomnia, which leads to a lack of energy, which leads to a lack of exercise, which leads to obesity, which leads to diabetes or a stroke or a heart attack. Debt is a slippery slope to poor mental health. Controlled debt is different; debt that has been carefully measured, meticulously researched, and thoroughly examined will help defer some of these mental health conditions.

DEBT IS A SLIPPERY SLOPE TO POOR MENTAL HEALTH.

I know from personal experience how this experience feels. With a $60,000 degree in education, and the average teacher pay at $35,000, it was going to take me at least 5-10 years to pay off my debt. With 5.5% interest, that amount would only grow while I worked, ate, payed for housing, purchased supplies, begged for early Christmas money, and forgot about vacations. As I write this, I still have about $15,000 in student loans to pay off, and every day, $3 to $5 dollars of that amount is tacked onto the bill in the form of interest. I have been out of school for close to six years now. And I'm technically doing well.

Other people, with way more debt than me, and with way worse jobs than me, have it worse. Mental health concerns are up to Threat Level 3AM, because that's probably the time they go to sleep at night. That's about the time I would go to sleep too, after worrying about how to pay all my bills. It's not pleasant, and saying it is not pleasant is the most egregious understatement I could make. My mind is metaphorically flipping me off and kicking me in the balls for the grave injustice of saying "it's not pleasant" does to me.

THE COST OF COLLEGE IS NOT JUST THE AMOUNT OF MONEY YOU WILL HAVE TO PAY.

Before you think about whether or not you want to go to college and if you are going to need to take loans out to pay for it. The cost of college is not just the amount of money you will have to pay. There is also time, energy, resources, relationships, and comfort. Be sure you can afford it before you spend it and be sure you don't borrow more than you can't pay back. College is a choice, and that choice comes with a bit of a risk. And it is a risk that you are ultimately responsible for, no matter the consequences.

There are ways to decrease the cost of college, and there are ways to pay for it. Student loans are, as I mentioned before, a popular road to take when it comes to paying for college. On (starting) average, the government will allow you to borrow around $20,000 a year to help pay for your time in school. This is enough to cover most tuition rates, any living expenses, and any additional fees or charges that come with the college price tag like the technology fee or the sports fee I mentioned earlier, and others such as parking tags, library accounts, registration fees, etc. The list goes on, and it varies by college and program.

College is a big life decision. You have to own it—I'm sure the Department of Education has laughed over my letter to them, in which I tell them that I have a right to free education. I still have to pay for that "right." And they will hound me until I do.

Debt is also another big decision. Don't screw it up.

CHAPTER RECAP:

1. The best way to avoid student loan debt is to AVOID it.
2. 2016 Student Loan Debt in America in 2016 = 1.3 trillion dollars – and it's only growing.
3. That's a lot of Big Macs.
4. The cost of college is not just financial. It's mental, emotional, and relational.

TAKEAWAY:

1. That's a lot of money! Count the cost before you decide whether or not to buy into college ideals.
2. Avoid McDonald's for lunch today. Diet, exercise, and mental health are all important.

CHAPTER 3: THE TRUTH ABOUT COLLEGE
Here's the Deal

I AM JUST GOING TO SAY IT, LIKE ALL THE other people I admire, even though I know some people are not going to like it: Not everyone is cut out for college.

Repeat: Not everyone is cut out for college.

REPEAT: NOT EVERYONE IS CUT OUT FOR COLLEGE.

And that's okay. It's *really* okay. You can be a happy, successful person and *not go to college*. You can make a lot of money and never need to go to college. You still have worth as a person, you can still get job training, and you can still learn a craft or skill or art or anything. There isn't some sacred part of life you're missing out on by not attending college.

Even so, there seems to be no end of people who will convince you that college is necessary. Parents, guardians, teachers, other students, salespeople, politicians,—all of these people sit on an imaginary jury of sorts, and they are all giving you the same verdict: "*GO TO COLLEGE!*"

SIDE NOTE: Please don't consider that subliminal messaging.

But — *but!* — all of these people are not you. *You* are in the best position to decide if college is something you want to pursue.

Your peers include many people who simply go to college because it's the "thing to do." Taxes are the "thing to do." College is optional, and it is your choice.

Your parents love you (I assume) and your teachers want to guide you (I assume), so it can be hard to find yourself at odds with others over the issue of your future. Others, like the politicians and the marketing companies, see you as a profit.

There are several reasons that there's so much debt in America; it's *not* just because a lot of people wanted to go to school and then the economy dropped. Many of the college recruiters who call you and the pretty brochures they send you are there to make you want to go to college. It works because there are a lot of legitimate reasons to go. But going to college might still not be the best option for you, and you have to be willing to stand up to any number of people who disagree with you, including salespeople. Many people who have student loan debt are people who wanted to change career fields, wanted higher pay, or wanted to look for better jobs and opportunities. These are the people who look at those brochures and take these calls with an end in mind. When you are not sure of what you want to be when you grow up, it can be easy to be swayed by the honeyed words of a salesperson who is paid on commission.

I can give you an example. I had a student who was three semesters into college when I talked with her. She wasn't sure of what she wanted to do, and when I asked her why she'd chosen to major in her field, she told me she wanted to change careers. I asked her which career she was looking at, and she *couldn't tell me*. Once I started talking to her, she found out that what she *really* wanted to do required a different degree.

Fortunately, she still had plenty of time to change programs, and it wasn't too much of a setback for her, but it was still unnerving. I know from personal experience how harrowing it can be to discover that you want nothing to do with your specialized field. I also know the pain of sucking it up and sticking in the field, even if you don't really like it. (I'm *good* at teaching, even if I don't like it that much.)

Some chapters ago, I told you to do your research on the college you are thinking about attending. Here's an even better place to begin: Yourself.

Research begins by asking questions (*not* making assumptions). So the first question you should ask is all about you.

KNOWING WHAT KIND OF PERSON YOU ARE, AND WHAT KIND OF JOB/WAY TO MAKE MONEY YOU WANT, DO YOU THINK YOU SHOULD GO TO COLLEGE?

Here's a list of all the possible answers to this question. Future chapters will dissect these answers in more detail:

1. **No**
2. **Not Yet**
3. **Yes (Variation One)**
4. **Yes (Variation Two)**
5. **Yes (Variation Three)**
6. **Yes (Non-traditional)**

Be warned: If you go to college, you will have to pay for it. If you take out loans, you will be expected to pay them back. There are some programs that will help you get your debt forgiven, but it's best to assume you will have to pay back any money you borrow, plus interest.

CHAPTER RECAP:

1. People will tell you what to do with your life.
2. Listen, but take your time in deciding if you're going to agree.
3. Don't buy into the hype of "right now, right here, make a decision." You have time.
4. Ask yourself if you think you should go to college, and be honest with yourself as you answer.

TAKEAWAY:

1. Pretty much the chapter recap.

CHAPTER 4: COLLEGE OPTION #1: NO
It's Okay Not to Go to College

I HAVE KNOWN ENOUGH STUDENTS, AND their parents, to be able to tell you that many parents today want their kids to go to college. And when many of them hear that their pwecious wittle baby doesn't want to go to college, they get worried. *It is okay to not go to college. Yes, really.*

IT IS OKAY TO NOT GO TO COLLEGE. YES, REALLY.

There are a lot of jobs that you can get right out of high school that will allow you to survive and save up for your future. Normally, people will ask me, *"Really?"* with one-arched eyebrow. I simply nod and tell them, "Yes." Or, if I am feeling more sarcastic, I ask them, "Where did Batman go to college?"

You have a lot of options, even if you decide not to go to college. There's working in sales, administration, construction, transportation, labor, or even working toward starting your own business in a field like media, art, or a trade. Some people will work online as freelancers, bloggers, or contractors. Another popular option is going into the military or working toward a family business position. Depending on your location, there are also options for working with companies over apps (Like Uber, for example).

There are several job training options. You can earn a certificate from a program that will allow you to enter into a career field in less than a year. Want to work in the medical field but don't want to go to college? Try starting out as a CNA (Certified Nursing Assistant) or a CMA (Certified Medical Assistant). There are training courses for a variety of jobs in many different fields; in the medical field alone, there are several options! These, while not providing you with a job, can give you an edge and some experience when it comes to finding professional work.

Job training can also be done on the job. For example, I have seen several photography jobs that involve working as an assistant. Photography is not the only career field you'll see realized in this way.

There are *plenty* of options for where to work, even if you don't go to college. Now, some jobs *do* require you to have a professional degree; if you are determined to pursue that line, you will end up going to college. Doctors, teachers, engineers, and scientists require a professional degree or higher in order to work or practice in the field. If you find yourself in this category, saying "No" to college is unwise.

CHAPTER RECAP:

1. It's okay if you don't want to go to college. *Really*.
2. Very few people seem to know where Batman went to college.

TAKEAWAY:

1. It's okay if you don't want to go to college, but you should have a plan (one besides "Marry rich" or "Win the lottery," please).
2. Make a plan to figure out what you want to do, and then what you need to do to achieve it.

CHAPTER 5: COLLEGE OPTION #2: NOT YET
Waiting on College

SINCE WE LIVE IN AMERICA, THERE ARE lots of opportunities to go to college. There are a huge number of colleges in America, and they offer many different programs. Several places have a reputation for specific programs: Harvard, for business, MIT for technology, UCLA for law, etc. Even if you can't get into the programs at those schools, there are universities that offer comparable teaching, if not experience and prestige. A lot of it comes down to money at that point. (I hate having to point this out but some countries, like Germany, will offer you college for free. But you have to score at a certain level on a barrage of tests for a lot of those. Besides, you'd likely have to be able to do it in German.)

Because you have a lot of options just from living here, you have the option of *waiting*. Waiting is not popular. Many people like to be sure of what they are doing, where they are going, and what choices they will make. With every choice you make, you are saying no to something else, and that is why you should understand your own reasons for not going to college right away.

Just like saying "No" to college, it *is perfectly okay to say you will wait on college,* and there are plenty of good reasons to do so. Here's a list of reasons to wait on going to college:

1. **If you are unsure of what major and/or job field you'd like to study.** There is no sense in rushing a decision if you might not have to rush it at all. I know some of my high school students started working during high school and got promotions working where they were. It paid more and they were still unsure about going to college, so they just stayed there. People know them, trust them, and they truly make a difference where they are. It's very nice to see, and they are happy. They also have no debt to get out of, so saving up for a down payment on a house or car has become much easier.

2. **If you want to experiment with your other job options first**. Again, there's no sense in putting money down for college if you don't have to. And you don't have to. You can get a regular job and see how it feels to be a member of the public working force.

    With this, you can also make your own opportunities. I had one student from my high school teaching years that started freelancing and found it made a lot of money for her, and she liked that because she could set her own schedule, and she didn't need a car or other transportation to drive anywhere (always a challenge for a 16-year-old.) She is currently working on saving up her freelancing money to buy a car and travel. She can still go to college later on. Several other students I have worked with apply to the military, too. This is an economic option because one of the benefits of going into the military is that you'll get a certain amount of college tuition covered through your service.

Some might want to travel to find work abroad; mission work, the Peace Corps, etc. There are plenty of options if you want to travel and work. Native English speakers sometimes find teaching jobs where they can work with students. One high school student I know of went to Africa to work at an orphanage and adopted a bunch of the kids there. She's doing well. And again, she has no debt.

3. **If you get married and want to start a family.** I know several people — some in my own family — who have held off college in order to pursue this path. Getting married is a big change, whether you realize it or not.

Having a family on top of that is even harder. Still worth it, but harder. There's no need to rush off to college if you want to have a family first. Several of my students have confirmed over and over again that they sometimes struggle with the family-work-school juggling act.

The best part of waiting to see if college is a good fit for you is that you'll be able to have some time to grow into "adulting," which is what all the cool kids are calling "growing up and taking responsibility for their own lives" on their silly memes.

Once you've had some time and lived your life a little, you'll be able see what you can do for school.

All of these options and examples are meant to encourage you. If you want to wait, you likely have a good reason to do so. Later on, you can still go to college when you've decided what you want to do.

YOU CAN STILL GO TO COLLEGE WHEN YOU'VE DECIDED WHAT YOU WANT TO DO.

The best thing about this is that you don't have to rack up debt in the meantime.

The first part of getting out of student loan debt was avoiding it. The second part of getting out of student loan debt is to make good decisions, so if you have to crawl into it, you won't drown.

CHAPTER RECAP:

1. It's okay if you don't want to go to college right away. You can always change your mind.
2. There are many reasons people don't want to go to college right away. And that's *fine*. You will still have options later, and you'll have the benefits of waiting, too—you'll be able to figure out what you want, you will have job experience, and/or some more financial sense from living in the "real" world (that strange place where so-called "Safe Spaces" don't exist unless you're visiting your mom.)
3. You might even have better motivations if you decide to wait for family reasons. There is nothing like having a child and a spouse depending on you to make you feel compelled to do your best. The extra support from the home front is nice, too. You're more likely to succeed if you have support. Waiting can also help you save up for college, so you don't have to take out as much money, thus helping you to avoid getting into more college debt.

TAKEAWAY:

1. Not sure about what you want to do? Don't stress. Waiting to see about college is okay.

CHAPTER 6: COLLEGE OPTION #3: YES, VARIATION ONE
Going Right Out of High School

IF YOU ARE CERTAIN OF WHAT YOU WANT to do with your life, especially when you're right out of high school, I sincerely applaud you. Many people don't grow up until they have to, and more and more people are finding ways to validate never growing up.

If you know what you want to do, you need a college degree to do it, and you didn't piddle around in high school so you are able to get into college without much extra trouble, you will say "Yes" to college.

Next, this is where the "good decisions" part comes up.

What makes a good decision?

There are plenty of things that people consider when looking at colleges. Popular concerns are:

1. Location
2. Price
3. Reputation
4. Program Availability
5. Food Plan
6. Job Opportunities/Career Services
7. Resources

SIDE NOTE #1: these are just general, popular concerns. They are not listed in any particular order.

I've worked with several students over the last six years, including high-schoolers looking to go to college, and college students who have no idea why they are in college, and these are the decision-making concerns that pop up the most. You might also have different concerns that are not listed here (i.e. "Is my best friend going to this college, too?").

Let's explore each of these topics, one by one,

1. **Location**

    Obviously, location is a concern if you want to stay at home and travel to school, or if you are working a part-time job while attending college. Very few people in school see long commutes between work and school as an "advantage." (Some grit their teeth and bear it regardless, but I've almost always seen these people fall asleep in class, oversleep, get caught in traffic, or have car issues.) If a close location to your home or family is a plus, see what you can do without compromising the other areas that are important to you.

2. **Price**

    This one is usually the top concern for many parents. Now that we've established that student loans can cause a lot of stress among American students, it's best to see if you can afford it, or at least how much you can afford to pay before you decide to take out loans.

SIDE NOTE #2: There are some tricks of the trade that can help you save money and get a better deal at college, which I'll talk about in later chapters.

The thing with price is that you want to make sure it is a good deal. You want to make sure that you get what you think you want: A degree in your chosen field, access to the right resources, networking opportunities to find jobs, internships and jobs coaching, and anything that will help you find or create your dream job—without losing everything that you have and more in the end—your time, your energy, your money, your pride, your dignity, your sanity . . . and so on and so forth.

In one sense, you could think of it like gambling where, if you are armed with the right knowledge and resources, it could turn into a big payout for the rest of your life.

3. Reputation

There are loads of reasons I hate sports. (Yes, I'm that kind of person. I already admitted I'm a teacher, so you should have known I'm not fun.) One of the bigger reasons I hate sports pertains to how certain colleges leverage their sports reputation against their academic reputation. If you are going to the school for its sports reputation, you should be one of the athletes they recruited. Otherwise, you might find yourself paying more than you need to—and that will probably translates into more debt.

SIDE NOTE #3: The trick for this one is to make sure that the college has the right reputation for what you want to do. It's no good to go to a school with a great reputation for lawyers if you're going to go for a medical degree. Of course, if you're going to Harvard because Natalie Portman went there, or you're going to Brown because Emma Watson went there, then that's another thing to consider. Don't go somewhere because of who's gone before you; you're going to college *for yourself*. You are a different person. You are also different from your ideal self (My ideal self is someone who is paid millions of dollars to sit around and think about how to make the world a better place while having the perfect body and perfect life, sipping on an ice-cold drink a million miles away from anyone else—though I'd still need a couple stores nearby or something. You can see where this is getting complicated, but you get the idea).

GO TO THE COLLEGE THAT WILL BEST SERVE YOUR FUTURE NEEDS, NOT YOUR CURRENT EGO.

Go to the college that will best serve your future needs, not your current ego. Even if you want a big-name school, you should have the academic performance and work ethic to back it up. There's a difference between confidence and arrogance, and most of it comes from whether or not your past experiences provide support to your present claims. If you want to go to Harvard, you better have the Harvard mindset, especially if you have to take out student loans to get there.

4. Program Availability

> This one is a no-brainer (but your brain is still required). If you want to be a marine biologist, it's probably not a good idea to look into the landlocked University of Nebraska for your college degree. Go where they have the program for the degree you are pursuing.

SIDE NOTE #4: Not sure which program you'd like to take? You can easily take a year (or two or even three) off before college, or you can opt for another variation of going to college. If you have no idea of what you'd like to do, then I'm sorry to have to tell you, but more research may be needed before you decide where you'd like to go to college. So go and take a few more quizzes on Facebook and Quizilla and Quizbuzz or whatever to help you figure out what career you would be good at *and* happy to do (not necessarily the same thing).

5. Food Plan

It's been said that the way to a man's heart is through his stomach, and many colleges have taken this approach when advertising to prospective students. While access to good food can be a blessed thing, don't make this a deal breaker. I didn't think having access to good coffee was essential until I graduated from college (I know, how naïve was I?!.) Point is, you can survive with bad food just as I did with bad coffee.

The good news is that if you don't like your college's food plan, they often have options (because most of the time a food plan is required) and there's likely a McDonald's or a Subway nearby (though, like I discussed earlier, you might want to stay away from the Big Macs). Or, you know, there could be a store nearby, or a friend's house. Or your mom's house. I think it's fair to say, if your mom doesn't want you to go far away for college she might use your college's food plan as an excuse to keep you at home, especially if she is a good cook.

6. Job Opportunities/Career Services

If a college provides help getting jobs post-college or even during college this is a solid reason to attend. Remember when there's talk of downsizing on NBC's *The Office*, and Andy Bernard starts talking about how Cornell University has a great Alumni group that helps their members get good jobs? That's the power of connections; Andy and his coworkers are facing the loss of jobs and income. Andy has an advantage over the rest of them: his Cornell University degree. Lesson learned here: if your dream job is out of reach, if your company is sold and heads down to Mexico, or if you have to train your replacement coming in on an HB-1 visa (yes, really), you might want to have a college ready to help you out in looking for new jobs.

SIDE NOTE #5: It's not just a new job that's important sometimes either. Some college career services will help you design your resume, coach you for interviews, and offer plenty of advice and training to give you an advantage over the competition.

Internships are also great chances to gain experience and learning credit. They can add some nice padding to your resume. Looking for a college that is well connected can help you in securing some of these opportunities.

7. Resources

Depending on what your field of study is, this consideration has a wide variety of possibilities. Going to the University of Miami for your marine biology degree allows you access to their beach and waterfront research labs. Going to Georgetown for a political science degree allows you to see the front lines of politics play because it's in Washington, D. C. Want to work in medicine? Emory University has a tight connection with Emory University Hospital (Imagine that). Bigger colleges often have the advantage here. But smaller colleges can have a lot of good resources, too.

One of the best of these resources is found in a library (that place where fussy old ladies keep books organized). Many college systems have access to research over virtual libraries. This resource is invaluable when you have to do a research project and you need quality, credible sources that Google might not have listed. In addition to these library services, some colleges offer tutoring, writing assistance, research labs, or focus groups or research projects.

SIDE NOTE #6: There are literally *hundreds* of examples I could give you for the benefits of having a college with good resources. Some offer seminars with popular, well-known, highly accomplished, (or "some-other-adjective") guest-speakers, great opportunities for learning aboard, community-based projects, and special courses or retreats for students.

The best thing I can tell you here is that the resources should complement your interests as well as your educational and career goals. This is logical and common-sensical, and it is your responsibility to make sure you use it to your advantage.

Once you have made it through your list of priorities, which may also include other items you want to consider, make your college selection and apply.

Then, once you have been accepted to a college, go there, get a dorm, sign up for your classes, buy your books, and stay there for four years or so. Then graduate, and you'll have your college degree!

After this, you can get a job or go to graduate school, where this process will more or less repeat itself.

If you take out student loans to pay for college, remember that you'll be paying those off after you graduate. You'll be paying for the time and experiences you have in college. As my dad says, "Make sure you get your money's worth."

CHAPTER RECAP:

1. If you want to work at a job that requires a college degree or higher, you'll need to go to college. Make sure your high school grades are good enough to get in, and you've taken all the required tests to get into the college you apply for.
2. When you apply to different colleges, make sure they have everything you're looking for.
3. If you have to take out student loans to pay for your education, make sure you make the most of college while you're there. You *will* have to pay back your loans.

TAKEAWAY:

1. If you're going to college after high school, earn good grades in high school, and take the courses you need to take.
2. Make sure you plan for college financially; this may include loans. Have your parents,

teachers, guidance counselors help if you need it.
3. High school is preparing you for college. It's not just a way to waste your time.

CHAPTER 7: COLLEGE OPTION #4: YES, VARIATION TWO
Getting the Basics Done First with Transfers, Community Colleges, & Associates Degrees

WE LIVE IN AMERICA, SO WE HAVE MANY options. That can make it hard to know what to choose; there are so many colleges in the country, and they all compete with to be on the "Best Colleges" lists, and scramble to be featured in magazines, newspapers, etc. It can be hard to get into a college, especially a high-ranking one that has a high tuition. Sometimes it can be really helpful to get credits in one place, and then transfer to your true college of choice.

For people who want to go to college after high school and pursue a degree, one idea is to start at a smaller college and then transferring credits to a larger university comes in.

More students have started going to community colleges for associate-level work, like math, English, and basic science classes. These can sometimes transfer to universities (though you'll have to make sure your credits will transfer beforehand) and then you can finish out the rest of your classes to earn your undergraduate degree.

Why do people attend a community college and then transfer to a university? Mostly for financial reasons. Transferring credits from a college that does not charge you as much as a larger college helps save on overall cost. With this method, you will attend a community college for usually the first two years of college, or about 60 credits worth of schooling. Many schools have a cap on how many credits they will transfer, and most average around 60 transfer credits. This will get you close to an associate degree, and you can then finish out the last two years or so of courses at a larger college.

Some advantages of this are easy enough to see: many community colleges offer transferrable credits to larger universities within their states. Many of these smaller colleges are closer to home, so you can easily live at home with the support of your family.

Some students who begin working before the end of high school are able to keep their jobs while they stay close to home while going to school at the community college. This allows students a better chance of building up their resumes and getting jobs somewhere else later on; if the student needs to move to attend a different college, getting a job will be easier with more experience.

While financial reasons are mostly behind choosing to start off at a community college, there are others, too. Starting at a community college can give you some time to work on figuring out your intended major, for example. If you're not sure what you want to do, but you want to go to college and take care of the general education courses while high school memories are still fresh scars on your mind, this is an excellent option.

It can also be a good idea to start at a community college if you are not sure if you would like to go to college at all. Getting a sample of college classes can help you get a better idea of what to expect should you decide you want to pursue a college degree.

Another point to reference here: Community colleges or smaller colleges often have great two-year programs. You can easily graduate with an associate degree instead of transferring. While it won't be the same as a bachelor's degree, there are several jobs that only require an associate degree that can give you a nice, steady income.

So, if you want a college degree, and you want to try to save on the cost, you can go to a community college or a smaller college for the first two years, and then transfer to a larger university or college to complete your degree, changing housing and job situations as needed. You can also graduate with an associate's degree and then, later on, you can go back to college to complete your bachelor's degree if you want.

While you will still have to pay for college, you can significantly cut down your bill by checking out the transfer credit options at smaller colleges.

CHAPTER RECAP:

1. If you want to save some money on college, consider going to a less expensive college. Community college is a great

option to help you get started on your college career.
2. Community colleges have a lot of two-year programs that can help you get your general education courses. You can then transfer to a larger university to finish out the degree.
3. You don't necessarily have to go to the community college to transfer credits. You can graduate with an associate degree.
4. If you have to take out student loans to pay for your college education, taking the community college route can save you some money. But you *will* still have to pay back your loans.

TAKEAWAY:

1. Check out a smaller college as a way to save on the costs of a college degree.
2. Transferring credits is a great way to help save money, but double-check the transfer credit options at the university you're transferring to for more information.
3. An associate's degree is another option that might work to your advantage if you want a degree but don't want as much debt. This will largely depend on your chosen field of study and the job market requirements.

CHAPTER 8: COLLEGE OPTION #5: YES, VARIATION THREE
Online College

ONE OF THE BEST THINGS ABOUT LIVING in this era is the many different ways that you can get educated. In the last few years, online college courses have popped up like dandelions during the first week of summer.

Keeping in mind the previous chapters' considerations—such as program availability, your chosen field of study, resources, services, etc.—you might want to consider completing your college work online. Plenty of people who have gone to traditional colleges have opted for a hybrid class (half-online, half-in person) to help with the work-life-school-family balance. Some people only take online classes for their degree.

The benefits of this are well documented. You have flexibility, you have pretty open communication with your professors, you have lots of resources (virtual libraries, online tutoring labs, eBooks) available to you, and you have it all available through the online platform.

In addition to having all your work available at your fingertips, you can also work and schedule the rest of your life around your school schedule. Many projects will have you engaging in your local community or even at your job for learning experiences.

Going to an online college will still cost money, but many students have found that the flexibility to learn on their own schedules is well worth the investment. Depending on the school, too, the online classes might not cost as much money.

While it is a different mode of schooling, the same principle applies with online classes as it does with the traditional brick and mortar schooling.: If you take out student loans, you will have to pay back the money. However, it can cut back on expenses, since you won't have to drive anywhere for classes, you can easily live at home, and you won't have room and board or a food plan to worry about.

CHAPTER RECAP:

1. If you want to save some money on college, consider online classes. This option will depend on your degree, but several general education courses can be delivered using the online platform.
2. If you have to take out student loans to pay for your online college education, you *will* still have to pay back your loans.

TAKEAWAY:

1. Online college might be a suitable option for you.

CHAPTER 9: COLLEGE OPTION #6: YES, NON-TRADITIONAL
Changing Your Mind about College

THE NON-TRADITIONAL ROUTE TO GO TO college is a newer trend. This route is largely taken by older people who started working after high school and want to go back to college now for a variety of reasons.

Non-Traditional students are people who want to learn a new trade or skill. Sometimes these are people who want to get a higher degree for their professional field, such as an entrepreneur who wants to officially get that business degree, even though he is self-employed. These students can have a degree in another subject, or they can be starting out for the first time. I've had students come back in order to get raises at work, I've had people come back so they could get paid more, find different jobs, learn about computers, because they're retired and bored or retired and need to go back to work, or just because they want to . . . yes, there *are* people who *want* to go back to school and learn new stuff.

Some of these people originally said "No," when it came to college. *It's okay to change your mind.* You can't have an ego when it comes to learning; there's no way to teach a know-it-all.

IT'S OKAY TO CHANGE YOUR MIND ABOUT COLLEGE.

Non-Traditional students are usually older, with years of life and work experience behind them. Because they are older than the students out of high school, they'll likely have more financial experience as well. That can be helpful when it comes to paying for college classes. They can qualify for scholarships and student loans, same as everyone else, and they can use some of the proactive methods listed in the next chapter.

CHAPTER RECAP:

1. If you originally didn't go to college, you can still change your mind.
2. If you have to take out student loans to pay for your college education, even after you've had years in the workforce, make sure you make the most of college while you're there. You *will* have to pay back your loans.

TAKEAWAY:

1. Saving money on college and getting out of debt is important at any age and any situation.

CHAPTER 10: PROACTIVE TIPS (NOT THE ACNE KIND)
Prepping and Paying for College

IF YOU HAVE DECIDED TO ATTEND A college, here are some tricks of the trade that, should you take advantage of them, will allow you to get a jumpstart on paying off any student loan debt you acquire during your education.

1. **AP Classes**

    Before you leave high school, there are plenty of things you can do to get ready for your college education (again, if that's something you would like to do). One route you can take to prepare for college, and even shorten your time there, is to take AP classes. These Advanced Placement courses offer a test at the end of the year, and if you receive a certain score, you can get college credit for the class. The scores range from 0-5, and most colleges will give you credit if you score a 4 or higher. Some will give you credit for less, and some, if you score a 5, will even give you an extra elective course credit. I have had students who have taken AP History, for example, and scored a 5 and they were given credit for American History and a History elective on their college transcripts. Taking high school courses and getting credit for them in college can save you a lot of time and money and worry!

If your school doesn't have the AP class for a certain subject, you can still see about dual enrollment or take CLEP exams.

2. Dual Enrollment

Some colleges and high schools will work together, allowing you to take college courses and high school courses at the same time. This is what dual enrollment does.

Not every high school will have this opportunity for you, but if you can get it, it might be something to consider.

I know someone who was dual enrolled in twelfth grade and took some college classes. By the time she was ready to actually go to college full time, she already had 13 credits. That's more than half a regular semester!

3. CLEP Exams

One of the easiest ways to save money on your college education is to take CLEP exams. CLEP is a registered company that works with CollegeBoard, which you will likely recognize from SAT, ACT, and AP Exams. They have a large amount of study materials, and once you get to college, if you want to "skip" taking a general education class, you will be able to choose from their list and sign up for a test. If you pass the test, you will get the credit for the class. That's a pretty good deal; most CLEP exams will cost close to $200, while a credit hour in an undergraduate class might be closer to $500 (and most undergraduate classes are between two and five credits).

With this one, it is a good idea to make sure you know which classes will be needed for your degree. Composition, for example, is a standard college class that nearly everyone has to take. If you have been given credit for this through AP classes, you can skip it. If you want to skip it but it has been a long time since high school, or if you did not take the AP class, you can take the CLEP exam. However, there are some degree requirements that will differentiate between something that seems like it would be the same, such as College Math and College Algebra. Make sure you sign up for the right test!

4. **Good Grades & Test Scores**

Getting good grades can also help. Many of my high-schoolers would qualify for a scholarship based on their GPA in school or their scores on college admission tests such as the SAT or the ACT. The nice thing about this is that the scholarships would often last for the year or even for the full time that the student is enrolled in the college. This leads into the next point, which includes . . .

5. **Scholarships & Grants**

These are chances for free money—money you don't have to pay back that you can put toward school. There are some that are specific to the college you select, and there are others that you can apply for no matter where you go to school (these are the ones you can Google more easily). From essays to majors to talents to stories to your family heritage, there are plenty of different types of scholarships out there you can apply for. There are some that ask you to make videos, send in a picture, write letters, play sports, design an advertisement, and several others things. Looking for grants will also yield similar results.

To help you through this endless field, ask a guidance counselor at your high school, or contact the financial aid office of your college once you've been accepted. They'll likely be able to direct you to where you need to look and give you tips on how to get ahead of the game.

6. **FAFSA**

   The FAFSA stands for the Free Application for Federal Student Aid. You can fill it out once you or your family receive your tax information for the previous year. This is how the US government can determine how much aid you're able receive for college. Some of these forms of aid include scholarships and grants, but more often than not they are loans. Your college will have more information on scholarships and grants, but your loan information from the FAFSA will likely be from the US government. They usually have the lowest interest rates, and they offer subsidized interest on many of their initial loan offerings. This is something that you will want to look at only after the other options are exhausted.

7. **Jobs with Student Benefits**

   Recognizing the importance of education, some companies have special programs for their student workers. You can look for a job that will help you pay for school, either in the form of tuition reimbursement or a scholarship. For this, you might need to see if any of these companies are close by, and if there are any openings. Some of the companies also require that you work there for a number of months or years before you can become eligible for their student benefits.

The big exception to this is the military. If you're accepted into the military, the US government will give you, as part of a benefits package, the ability to pay back loans or to pay for higher education. Some of my military friends and students have done just this. Be sure to check requirements for this one, too, however; some of my students, if they failed classes, were not allowed to use the money they'd gotten from the military to pay for the class (they had to pay for it out of their own pockets).

8. **Personal Responsibility: Finances**

This is the one people tend to have a problem with—taking personal responsibility for your finances. This means knowing your income (if any), possibly getting an income, budgeting, anticipating loan payments, looking for extra work, recognizing the lottery is not going to solve all your problems, etc. If you know you are going to want to go to college and you are working to save some money for it, the best time to begin is now. You can easily get your parents or family or even some friends to help keep you accountable, and you might even find that you have people who are willing to help.

Learning how to manage your finances while you're young can really help you live a better life in the long run. Even if it's a pain, you will learn one way or another. Since this is in the "proactive" chapter, I'm hoping that you will learn it before experience teaches you the hard way, or life in general just seems to get in the way.

CHAPTER RECAP:

1. See whole chapter, as needed.

TAKEAWAY:

2. See chapter recap.

CHAPTER 11: REACTIVE TIPS (NOT THE RADIOACTIVE KIND)
Tips & Tricks

IF YOU ARE READING THIS BOOK IN HOPES of getting insight into what will help you now that you are finished with school, I don't want to leave you hanging. The best thing to do in a bad situation is find a way out of it—some people would complain about it, and I don't think that is very helpful, especially since, with loans, *you* signed up for them and you, theoretically at least, knew you were going to have to pay them back. (I warned you about that.) Here's a list of things that you can do once you have graduated from college and you have student loans to pay back:

1. **Budget, Budget, Budget**

    Knowing where your money goes is the first step to knowing how to make it go to the right places. Keep a budget of your expenses and your bills, making sure you know how much you need to pay on your student loan each month. The best time to start doing this is now, of course, but you also have a grace period of six months after you graduate, where you are not required to put money down toward your student loan debt. It is important to remember that, during this time, the interest on your student loans will continue to accrue, so if you can (not if you *want*), begin paying them back immediately. Several of my college students are already doing this while they are in school. Interest doesn't always seem like a lot, but 5% of 100 is 5, so for every $100 of debt, you'll have to pay an extra $5. Considering the likelihood of spending at least $30,000 on college, that's a lot of extra $5 payments.

2. **Income-Based Loan Repayment Options**

If you are strapped for cash, or you have graduated and you don't yet have a job, the US government will allow you to select a repayment plan based on your income. This can take your payments per month down to around $50, even if they started around $500. If you have a family and dependents, you might even be able to change it to less than $50 a month.

Again, the trick here is to watch the interest. If you can afford more than $50 a month, it is best to pay it down. The interest on a loan is what will make you cringe in the end. Contacting your loan provider (Department of Education, Navient, etc.) will allow you to explore further options for this; there is nothing you can do to get out of paying your loan other than fulfilling the terms of your loan agreement. Even declaring bankruptcy will not work; student loans are the rare exception to this.

3. Public Service Loan Forgiveness

While I have mentioned that you need to make sure you are aware that you will have to repay your student loans, there are some ways that it is possible to escape this fate. However, it is only for a select few, and it is not guaranteed. If you work at a not-for-profit, or for a government agency, or in public services, such as social workers, teachers, and nurses, it is possible to have some of your loans forgiven based on your time working.

In addition to this possibility, there are companies like AmeriCorps and Teach for America that will give its designated workers a stipend for their student loans while they work. You can easily look into these companies to see where they have openings for jobs.

4. **Jobs & Side Gigs**

   Just like there are some companies that will give you some student benefits, there are some companies that are now working with their employees to help them repay their student loans. These companies are rare at the moment, but will likely increase in the future as many people see this as a favorable trait in a business.

   In addition to these jobs, many people who are serious about repaying their loans as fast as possible turn to picking up side jobs. Getting a second job can also be a great way to find new interests and help expand your business or skill set; I know of some people who used their side jobs as a way to start their own businesses later on.

5. **Refinancing**

   When all else fails and you are stuck in a tenuous situation when it comes to repaying your loans, you can look into companies like Student Loan Hero to help you refinance your loans. This usually means combining them into one easy payment for a longer timeframe or getting a better interest rate.

Some of my students have had good experiences with this, and others have had bad experiences. Make sure you check to make sure that the companies are real and credible. The US government has put out a warning in recent years about fraudulent companies who are taking advantage of people who want to repay their loans.

CHAPTER RECAP:

1. See whole chapter, as needed.

TAKEAWAY:

3. See chapter recap.

CHAPTER 12: CLOSING STATEMENTS

COLLEGE IS, LIKE MANY THINGS IN LIFE, A choice. It's a choice that doesn't come easily or without sacrifice; it's not a choice that should be made lightly or by your parents or peers. Making choices is sometimes hard because we don't want to make the wrong ones, and we don't want to feel bad if we do. That's the price of freedom: personal responsibility.

So, how do you deal with student loan debt in America? Short of death, or becoming a permanent ex-pat, you will have to pay back the loans that you borrowed for college. Here is my quick review:

1. AVOID getting into student loan debt in the first place. So have a plan and a backup or two.
2. PLAN ahead for debt. Your parents, family, etc. can all work to raise and save money for you. Once you've decided to go to college, you can start saving up for it as well.
3. BE PROACTIVE. Find ways to get college credits for less money, find scholarships, grants, or opportunities that will pay for your college education, find a job that will cover tuition or book costs, and find ways to save money on supplies.
4. IF you have to be reactive, work out a plan and stick to it, changing it as needed. This

includes budgeting, saving up money during school and your grace period (if you borrowed from the US government), and finding ways to pay off your loans faster or refinancing through another company.

It can be hard, but there is hope. Even if you make the wrong choices, and feel bad about it (as I did), you can use it to help other people have better lives (as I am doing in writing this). Should you go to college? Yes or no, or not yet. The choice is yours. The debt you incur while you're there might not be worth the trouble if you make your decision too fast or too flippantly. Or if that zombie apocalypse ever comes to pass, though with about 2/3 of America on sleeping aids, I'm not sure it isn't already here. Rage culture is getting to be a big thing too.

People wonder where America is going sometimes, and all I can say to that is: you have control over exactly one person in the whole country. Yourself. So take care of yourself. Do your research (notice I didn't say "homework"), make your choices, and own up to them in the end. If everyone took care of their own problems, we wouldn't have any problems left. And if someone is struggling with his or her problems, reach out and help them directly (don't just go to Uncle Sam). If you believe in "Karma," you might think helping them would be a good move. Helping them now might be preventing something adverse for you or others in the future, it will make that person feel better, *and* it will make you feel good, too. Really. *Really.*

REALLY.

While I don't believe in karma (personally, I think karma is for pussies; give me poetic justice any day of the week), it is not a bad idea to "name drop" it here so I can manipulate you into being a better person.

The choice of going to college or not is up to you. It depends on your interests, your drive, and your options. Don't let getting student loans deter you if you think it is worth it, but don't get caught up in despair if you find out it's not. Either way, there is nothing stopping you.

There is nothing stopping you from learning, there is nothing stopping you from trying, and there's nothing stopping you from being a better person *right now.*

THERE'S NOTHING STOPPING YOU, AND THERE'S NOTHING STOPPING YOU FROM BEING A BETTER PERSON *RIGHT NOW.*

ABOUT THE AUTHOR

C. S. JOHNSON is the award-winning, genre-hopping author of several novels, including young adult sci-fi and fantasy adventures such as the Starlight Chronicles series, the Once Upon a Princess saga, and the Divine Space Pirates trilogy. She has written articles for The Rebelution, MTL Magazine, Hollywood in Toto, StudioJake, and more. With a gift for sarcasm and an apologetic heart, she currently lives in Atlanta with her family. Find out more and subscribe to her newsletter mailing list at http://www.csjohnson.me.

AUTHOR'S ACKNOWLEDGEMENTS

EDITOR

Jennifer C. Sell

Jennifer Clark Sell is a professional book editor and proofreader. She works from her home in Southern California. With her years of professional and personal experience, she offers several quality packages for authors. Find her at https://www.facebook.com/JenniferSellEditingService.

Photo Credit: Savannah Sell

AUTHOR'S ACKNOWLEDGEMENTS

EDITOR

Faith K. Moore

Faith K. Moore is a freelance writer with publications in venues like The Wall Street Journal, The New York Daily News, and The Federalist. She also contributes regularly at PJ Media and Evie Magazine. Her self-published book, *Saving Cinderella*, is available online. Before becoming a writer, Faith taught writing and other subjects to elementary school students. Find her at https://www.faithkmoore.com.

Photo Credit: Faith K. Moore

AUTHOR'S NOTE

Thank you for reading this book, or at least skipping to the end; pretty sure I get paid either way, unless you return it after reading it, in which case you will suffer loss for that in heaven. Here's the part where I beg you to leave reviews.

PLEASE LEAVE A REVIEW FOR THIS BOOK!

Help get the word out about this book. Please leave a review and say something nice.

SERIOUSLY, YOU'VE PROBABLY PRAISED YOUR DOG FOR POOING MORE THAN WHAT I'M ASKING YOU TO DO WHEN YOU LEAVE A REVIEW.

IT'S NOT HARD. GIVE IT THE OLD COLLEGE TRY, MAYBE?

REVIEWS ARE THE BLOODLINE OF BOOK SALES. DONATE AND SAVE THIS BOOK'S LIFE TODAY!

LEAVE A REVIEW AND I'LL GIVE YOU EXTRA CREDIT.

FORWARD THIS BOOK TO 10 PEOPLE AND LEAVE A REVIEW AND EITHER NOTHING BAD WILL HAPPEN TO YOU OR SOMETHING GOOD WILL HAPPEN TO YOU OR MAYBE NEITHER BUT YOU'LL MAKE OTHERS HAPPY SO THAT'S GOOD.

PICK ONE OF THE PERSUASIVE LINES ABOVE AND THINK ABOUT THE BEST ONE WHILE YOU LEAVE A REVIEW!

I hope you've enjoyed reading this much more than I enjoyed writing it. Writing all this down was unpleasant, but that's what happens when you try to make the world a better place; it demands that you sacrifice something of yourself, and goodness knows time is my most precious asset.

Oh well.

Your Loving Teacher,

Mrs. Johnson

www.ingramcontent.com/pod-product-compliance
Lightning Source LLC
Chambersburg PA
CBHW052042280426
43661CB00085B/63

9 781948 646642